A CONVERSATION
WITH JESUS

ON

SUFFERING

A CONVERSATION
WITH JESUS

ON

SUFFERING

DAVID HELM

CHRISTIAN
FOCUS

Scripture quotations are from *The Holy Bible, English Standard Version*, copyright © 2001 by Crossway Bibles, a publishing ministry of Good News Publishers. Used by permission. All rights reserved. ESV Text Edition: 2011.

ISBN 978-1-5271-0326-9

Published in 2019

by

Christian Focus Publications Ltd.,
Geanies House, Fearn, Ross-shire,
IV20 1TW, Great Britain

www.christianfocus.com

Cover design and typeset by: Pete Barnsley (CreativeHoot.com)

Printed in China

CONTENTS

TWO WORDS
BEFORE
BEGINNING

ONE

The book in your hands is one of six. Short volumes all. Think of them as people to meet, not pages to be read. In each, a charcoal sketch is drawn of a person who first appeared on the pages of John's Gospel. Both women and men. Real flesh and blood. All worthy of attention. And each one fully capable of standing on their own two feet.

Beyond this, they all have someone in common. Jesus. The Nazarene. The Christ— he who forever changed the world we live in. Anyway, they all met him. In person. And they talked with him. More than that. Each one had a *conversation with Jesus* about something important to them.

TWO

I suppose something should be said about why 'these six'? Let's just say the selection is subjective. Author's prerogative. I liked them. I wanted to know them. And I learned significant things from each one of them. There are good reasons to think that you will connect with them too. Their struggles are our struggles. Their questions too. In fact, some people are saying there has never been another century to resemble the one these six lived in, until ours came along. And if that is the case, you may just run into yourself by running into them.

At any rate, there came a day when they all ran into Jesus. Of course, he is the only character to emerge in every encounter. I am confident that you will enjoy getting to know him.

DIRECTOR'S
NOTES

CAST:

※ **MAN:** middle aged, but much older in looks, an invalid, unkempt

※ **JESUS:** a known miracle worker, direct, commonly attired

※ **RELIGIOUS LEADERS:** pious, well heeled, but visibly unhappy

SETTING:

The city of Jerusalem. An urban pool near the Sheep Gate. The area is densely populated, but not by people of means. The forsaken are here. The sick. The diseased. The suffering masses. Weakness. Putrid smells. Heat. And shelter? Only for those crowded under Herod's colonnades.

The opening scene demands a drone or an aerial camera. First hovering. Then moving, until, at last, plunging in among the hopeless multitude. The camera glides quickly under the standing colonnades, and then steps in and among the gruesome and the bizarre. Always avoiding contact with those at its feet. Odors of illness rise.

The pool itself is now in sight. Only one man is in focus. His body is curled up on the ground. He is clearly in the kind of agony that long ago stopped him from crying out.

A CONVERSATION WITH JESUS ON
SUFFERING

Affliction makes God appear to be absent for a time, more absent than a dead man, more absent than light in the utter darkness of a cell. A kind of horror submerges the whole soul. During this absence there is nothing to love. What is terrible is that if, in this darkness where there is nothing to love, the soul ceases to love, God's absence becomes final.

—WAITING FOR GOD[1]

The Jewish calendar was drawing to a close. It was the day before Rosh Hashanah and thousands of prisoners at Auschwitz were gathering for a service of sung prayers. Among them was a fifteen-year-old boy. He stood apart from the rest. He was alone, yet not without his thoughts.

What are You, my God? I thought angrily. How do you compare to this stricken mass gathered to affirm to You their faith, their anger, their defiance? What does Your grandeur mean, Master of the Universe, in the face of all this cowardice, this decay, and this misery? Why do You go on troubling these poor people's wounded minds, their ailing bodies?.... these men whom You have betrayed.[2]

BETRAYED BY GOD

That fifteen-year-old boy's name was Elie Wiesel. He would later become a Nobel Prize winner for his ability to convey in words what the world needed to know about the atrocities of war, human hatred, evil, and the numbing effect the sufferings of his people ended up having on his view of God.

When it comes to suffering, this pervasive sense of divine betrayal is felt by many. Perhaps you are even one or them. And if so, let me say that your sense of being betrayed by God is entirely understandable. I am sorry for what you have gone, and are going, through. I know that I can't begin to identify with the sufferings experienced by some who are now reading this short book. Even my closest approximations would fall woefully short. Human suffering raises many questions for us all. Not the least of which is the one pondered most of all: the problem of evil.

SUFFERING AND THE QUESTION OF 'FIRSTS'

Put simply, where does evil come from? How did it *first* arrive on the scene? What set it in motion? The question is primarily one of origins, and a fair treatment of it would require a book of its own. You won't find that here. This book is devoted to the personal and experiential offshoot of that larger theme (which is generally more impersonal and philosophically treated). Here we want to look at a human suffering, and not from the vantage point of a classroom. That said, before devoting our time to the man at the pool and his conversation with Jesus, perhaps it is worth at least putting our toe in the water on the dilemma of evil.

The Bible itself does not tell us precisely how evil first entered the world or from where it originates. Across the centuries, theologians and philosophers haven't been able to pin it down, not at least to anyone's complete satisfaction. We have learned though, that the problem of evil is unlike the existence of God. Evil has an origin, a beginning, and God does not. When it arrived, and through whom, remains a secret. Hidden. Sealed up in the mysterious mind and plan of God. In the book of Genesis, the presence of the wicked serpent in the Garden of Eden is a given. But, where it originated from, is left unanswered.

Also, we know that things like human suffering and affliction are extensions of the presence of evil, and that their sources are many. Natural disasters still bring havoc on the world.

Diseases are often carried from one person to another, while other times genetics alone plays the determining role in our suffering.

At the same time, humanity cannot be excluded as a source of evil. Something is wrong with our nature. We are all sinful (or flawed people with often selfish and evil intentions) and each of us possesses the capacity to inflict harm on others. The origins of human pain and suffering do appear to be numerous. Simply put, the world is not right. It is not as it should be. It remains a far cry from that moment in the garden when God looked on all that he had made and pronounced it 'very good.'

Interestingly though, while no religious viewpoint has a comprehensive answer for the origin of evil, Christianity does offer a solution to its persistence. According to John's Gospel, this same Jesus (who will converse with the man at the pool) will later conquer the insistent grip evil holds on us—and he will do so, paradoxically, through *suffering* on a cross. How ironic. The problem of evil will be beaten back by the agent of suffering, the very thing it inflicted upon us in its day of power. There, in his death and resurrection, Jesus will defeat death and, according to John, offer eternal life to all who believe in him.

Further, and to our great relief, the Bible goes on to say that this same Jesus will come again to eradicate evil once and for all, in all its forms, including its tyranny of darkness. While we may not be entirely satisfied with our understanding of the origins of evil, the gospel does inform us about its temporal nature and ultimate defeat. And that should be a consolation worth pondering.

OTHER QUESTIONS TOO…

If you picked up this book looking for more, a full and robust philosophical treatment on the problem of evil and its origins, you can set this one down now. It won't be coming. But perhaps you picked up this book for experiential reasons instead. Some of us are suffering greatly, or know a friend or family member who is going through something that is shaking the very foundations of life, including, but certainly not limited to, Christian faith. You may find yourself in a tough spot, or you may know someone who is asking other questions related to suffering. 'Where was God in the darkest hour of my life? Where was he when it mattered most? Why was God seemingly absent at important and heart-wrenching times? Why this illness? And pain? Can anyone explain to me why God remains hidden from view?'

Suffering, on the other hand, always seems to be on display. It is easy to spot. Sickness arrives out of nowhere, and without warning. Real lives, even the lives of loved ones, are destroyed out in the open for all to see. The result is a sense of being betrayed by God— plagued by a gnawing sense of divine neglect.

Given this set of questions, we are right to

ask: 'Where does a person go for help when dealing with human suffering? Is there, perhaps, someone we can talk to?'

Here, we get the benefit of listening in on someone's very real conversation about suffering. This conversation puts us within the sound of Jesus' own voice. And equally, we hear from one who can personally identify with the line quoted from Wiesel at the start: 'these men here…whom you have betrayed.'

THE MAN AT THE POOL

The gospel of John presents just such a person.[3] This man had been subject to a protracted and excruciating life of suffering. And he is asking questions we would like to see Jesus address. For centuries we have simply known him as the man at the pool. When we meet him, he is presented like this:

Now there is in Jerusalem by the Sheep Gate a pool, in Aramaic called Bethesda, which has five roofed colonnades. In these lay a multitude of invalids— blind, lame, and paralyzed. One man was there who had been an invalid for thirty-eight years.

John gives us an urban scene. The sheer number of people astound us. And the varied nature of their sicknesses startles us. Given a choice, we would leave the decomposition and decay of this place behind. But, no, John won't allow it. He focuses our attention on one man. He wants us to take notice. And we do. Our eyes fall upon him among the many. And we lament. For we are told that the man at the pool has been an invalid for thirty-eight years.

Not many of us are familiar with looking at the unrelenting persistence of human suffering. But here we are. The place John has led us to resembles an outdoor hospital ward, but one without doctors, nurses, medication, or therapy. The moans of the sick are unsettling. Most don't even bother to look up at us at all.

This man doesn't. And why should he? Thirty-eight years, without a single step taken on his own.

Because I don't know much about this kind of thing, I asked a doctor, a friend of mine, what happens to the body after being an invalid for that length of time. She told me that the lower limbs would atrophy, and with the loss of muscle they would almost look withered. He would be flexed at the hips and knees. And depending on the care he was receiving, he could have some pretty foul-smelling sores. Worse yet, he may even suffer from incontinence. Needless to say, he would have appeared quite ill.

If ever there was a man who had reason to feel betrayed by God, surely this man did. The tyranny of darkness had, by the time Jesus met him, possessed a powerful grip over his body for nearly four decades. Here is a man, if allowed to speak, from whom there is much to learn.

THE FIRST ENCOUNTER

Now, imagine that we are not walking alone. Jesus—the one John claims to be the light of the world—is following right behind. Through the sick and the dying, he too presses on. He joins us, and now stands with us beside that man at the pool. Suddenly, and without warning, he plunges straight away into the subject of this man's sufferings with the oddest question of all:

> When Jesus saw him lying there and knew that he had already been there a long time, he said to him, 'Do you want to be healed?'

What a strange thing to say. The words, 'Do you want to be healed?' are entirely unexpected. *Do you want to be healed?* Of course, he does. Who wouldn't? Jesus' conversation starter on the subject of human suffering comes as a complete shock and surprise. His question appears quite insensitive. Some might even call it hurtful. Can you imagine asking an unemployed man on the street if he would like a well-paying job? Or an injured athlete if she would like to compete? Or a dying child if he would like to live a long life? Absurd. On every level. Therefore, what are we supposed to do with this opening line? What could Jesus possibly mean? Perhaps hearing the man's response will illuminate things for us.

> *The sick man answered him, 'Sir, I have no one to put me into the pool when the water is stirred up, and while I am going another steps down before me.'*

The opening words from the man at the pool only seem to complicate matters. At least for us. They don't shed light on Jesus' meaning (if Jesus' conversation starter is going to make sense, it will have to come later in the dialogue). The man's words are strange. What is this talk about the water being stirred up? Is he saying he would have been healed a long time ago if he'd been put into it?

Some explanation is in order. We can be helped by a knowledge of some background. In some early manuscripts of John's Gospel, we find additional details which indicate that 'an angel of the Lord went down at certain seasons into the pool, and stirred the water: whoever stepped in first after the stirring of the water was healed of whatever disease he had.' Knowing this is useful. It helps us make some sense of the man's response. Whether the story surrounding the occasional attendance of angels at the pool was true, or merely the stuff of legend, we will never know. But this much is clear, in the ancient city of Jerusalem, at the pool by the Sheep Gate, there was a place with a mystical quality, just as certain places today continue to attract people hoping to be cured.

It seems, though, that the man appears to be venting a bit too. Perhaps Jesus' question didn't sit too well with him? After all, his words reveal a hint of bitterness—bitterness for having gone so long without healing. They could be interpreted as: 'Nice question! So, do you think I just like laying here? The deal is, I'm all alone in this rotten world. I've got no one to help me. No one looks out for me. Others always get ahead of me.' The fact of his bitterness should not surprise us. It is simply another consequence of feeling betrayed by God. But where the conversation goes after this odd opening and exchange is even more surprising.

SOME SURPRISING STEPS

Abruptly, and without any warning, Jesus surprises the man again. Instead of expressing sympathy for him, or offering to help in some way, he simply looks him squarely in the eyes and says:

'Get up. Take up your bed and walk.' And at once the man was healed, and he took up his bed and walked.

Jesus spoke a command. It was no longer a conversation. 'Get up. Take up your bed and walk.' And with it, the discussion we hoped to have with Jesus on human suffering seems to be over. The man, having taken Jesus at his word, is now a walking miracle for all to see, replacing the need for speech (at least that is how it appears at this point).

It is difficult for us to fully capture the scene. Multiple camera angles have trouble taking it all in. After thirty-eight years, the man is on his feet. He appears as surprised as the rest of us. Tucking his bed roll under his arm he is now standing! And with new found strength in his legs, he begins putting them into motion. At first, his steps are deliberate. But then, with his confidence rising, he excitedly moves, leaping over and among the multitudes. His shouts are those of song, and the melody is sweet. 'I can walk! I can walk! I have been healed!'

SUFFERING AND THE QUESTION OF FAIRNESS

Before chasing the man down, however, we need to take a step back. After all, his physical healing raises a significant question for us. This question has many sides and it can be expressed in a number of ways. For example, if Jesus is who John claims, then why didn't he heal everyone at the pool on that day? Or, to put it slightly differently, why does this man at the pool get relief from his sickness when others must bear their afflictions to the end? Is that even *fair*? To put a more personal angle on it: 'Why doesn't God choose to heal me, or my loved ones, when others seem to get over their seasons of suffering?' These are significant questions. They are not merely philosophical—but deeply personal. If our first question was concerned with the origins of evil, this second one seems to be centered on the apparent partiality of Jesus in healing.

The issue of Jesus, a known miracle worker, exercising partiality on the issue of human suffering, is a colossal thing to consider. After all, you will be far less likely to believe in Jesus if his power to help is arbitrary and without a genuine concern for *all* people. What are we to make of this?

For starters, we should not be ashamed to admit that we simply don't *fully* know why Jesus would pass over the multitudes on this day and heal only this one man, just as we don't understand the apparent randomness in people recovering from illnesses today. What we do know from the Bible however, is this: According to the gospel of John, Jesus' primary purpose in coming into the world was to save us from our sins, not from all our sicknesses. Perhaps this accounts for why he didn't, and doesn't, heal everyone?

An illustration might help bring the idea into sharper focus. Imagine, for a moment, that Jesus lived today and that he had the power to heal. But also keep in mind that he had come to save us from an eternity of suffering in hell. Naturally, once news got out that he possessed power to alleviate our earthly seasons of suffering, he would gain incredible fame. He'd be bigger even than any athlete, musician, or movie star. In fact, from every corner of the earth, people would travel to see him. But, and this is worth remembering, if his stated purpose in coming was to get to the root of all evil, even to conquer death on our behalf, then he would need to accomplish something greater even than physical healing. He would need to concern himself supremely with humanity's universal sickness: sin. He would need to provide spiritual health.

According to the message of the Bible, this is the very thing Jesus did. He came to earth and suffered on the cross in our place. In doing so, he put evil to death. So, according to the Bible, Jesus' concern for humanity is not partial. Because he never sinned, he accomplished something great for us all and those who believe in him will one day walk on their own two feet into everlasting life.

I am aware that you might not be in a place where the above answer meets with your present frame of mind. We are complex creatures. The emotional pain that attends the sufferer is carried to the end. And that weight can be as immense as the physical duress one experiences. Believe, me, I am not trying to push all those realities under the rug with Christian niceties. Platitudes. As though a single line on the love of Jesus will solve our distress overnight.

It doesn't. I know. In fact, I know such a man. His wife possessed an inner beauty, yet her body was afflicted with tumors. And although she fought hard against cancer's advance, eventually, she wasted away. Death won out. At her funeral, her husband would not have the biblical account of Christ's resurrection read aloud. Even though he had once attended church. 'Not here. Not now.' Not at her funeral. For him, at that time anyway, the biblical notion that God is good was simply too much for him. That said, in time, and over time, I continue to trust that the promises of God, as made known in the work Christ accomplished for us all, will one day bring comfort to him, and to you, both in this life and the next.

THE ALLEVIATION OF SUFFERING CREATES QUITE A STIR

Evidently, the healing of the man at the pool created quite a stir (unlike the kind purportedly made by angels on the water). People on every side were thrown into a state of confusion. And a bit of controversy developed. John tells us why:

Now that day was the Sabbath. So the Jews said to the man who had been healed, 'It is the Sabbath, and it is not lawful for you to take up your bed.' But he answered them, 'The man who healed me, that man said to me, "Take up your bed, and walk."' They asked him, 'Who is the man who said to you, "Take up your bed and walk"?' Now the man who had been healed did not know who it was, for Jesus had withdrawn, as there was a crowd in the place.

A few things are worth mentioning from the interaction between the man and the religious leaders. First, shortly after the healing, they must have seen the man dancing through the streets with his bed all rolled up. Normally, this wouldn't attract much attention. But because it was the Sabbath, as John makes us aware, such an act was considered to be work. In Judaism, the Sabbath was the day of rest.

Some religious leaders of that time taught that *rest* included the idea of not spending your day *running* all over town! And it isn't hard to envisage them now—piously frowning and taking issue with the very thing this man set off to do. But who can blame the man?

The second, and more important observation from these verses is that in all the excitement surrounding the healing, the man couldn't even tell them who it was that healed him! While he danced for joy, Jesus simply withdrew from sight. In the chaos, Jesus never had the chance to say anything more to the man, nor the man to Jesus.

A SECOND ENCOUNTER

What are we to make of that? Didn't Jesus want a conversation with the man at the pool on suffering? Are we to believe that Jesus didn't care to reveal his real mission to the man? I find that highly doubtful. Or, did Jesus intend to find the man later, after things calmed down, so he could take up a conversation on the man's relationship to God? What we want is that very thing.

Fortunately for us, it appears that a second encounter was what Jesus had in mind. A scene change is underway. The pool recedes from view. Finding the man is the only issue now. Where might the man go? What would you do on the first day in thirty-eight years that you could do whatever you wanted and go wherever you pleased? I don't know where I would have gone, but we know where this man went, and Jesus knew where to find him.

John writes, 'Afterward, Jesus found him in the temple...' Wow! Imagine that. The early steps of this man, long bound to feelings of betrayal, were those which brought him into the house of the Lord. Was he considering a return to a relationship with God? Was he an ardent believer, a man of genuine faith, who now had a chance to offer his thanks properly? And if so, does Jesus merely want to commend him for his years of faithful testimony even under the most difficult of circumstances? In other words, is the man's presence in the temple asking us to consider the possible relationship human sufferings have with our spiritual wellbeing?

SUFFERING AND THE QUESTION OF SPIRITUAL SOUNDNESS

The ongoing narrative begins to provide us with something of an answer:

> *Afterward Jesus found him in the temple and said to him, 'See, you are well! Sin no more, that nothing worse may happen to you.'*

By setting down these words into the conversation, it would appear that Jesus does make something of the man's sufferings and his wellbeing—his *spiritual soundness*. But for us to begin making sense of it, we will need to observe something imbedded in the discourse. Not only in what Jesus says here, but by comparing it to what he first said at the time their conversation began.

Here Jesus states, 'See, you are *well!* Sin no more, that nothing worse may happen to you.' But back at the beginning he had asked him 'Do you want to be *healed*?' That question, the one with which Jesus opened, perplexed us at the time. Remember? We weren't quite sure how to handle it. We thought it was hurtful, or, at least, a very strange way to begin the conversation.

Interestingly, and this is important for us to take in now, the same Greek word, translated *healed* at the start of their conversation, happens to be the word translated *well* in this final exchange. Certainly, the man would not have missed the connection! Stack the two lines together and they could read like this:

* 'Do you want to be made *well*?' (We took this to relate only to his physical condition.)

* 'See, you are *well*! Sin no more, that nothing worse may happen to you.' (Jesus relates this word to his spiritual condition.)

The importance and implications of this observation may take time to settle in. Consider for a moment that Jesus' first question might have more in mind than the man's physical healing. What if he was asking 'Do you want to be made well, by that I mean in the fullest sense of the term—both physically and spiritually?' This could make sense. And this is especially the case if it can be shown that he is using the same word again now, in the temple, in reference to a spiritual warning.

Supposing this for a moment, we are now in a position to more fully appreciate the intent of Jesus' odd way of beginning the conversation. What he actually asked the man was this: 'Do you want to be made well? That is, do you want to be set straight spiritually, or just physically? Do you want a relationship with me and with my Father? And if so, are you prepared to take up the moral obligations that come along with that? After all, they are more demanding than taking up that mat. Are you ready for all that?'

If this take on the conversation is right, and I think it is (more on why in a bit), then you and I need to pause and do some serious reflecting on human suffering, spiritual health, and what it all means for us to carry on our lives in relationship to God.

SUFFERING AND THE QUESTION OF FAULT

But let's begin first by addressing the most immediate and potentially troubling implication. This line that Jesus uses—'*Sin no more...*'—seems to directly connect *this* man's illness with his sin. As though Jesus was tying his thirty-eight years as an invalid to divine retribution for something he did wrong. Can this be so? Is human suffering ever the consequence of divine discipline? Can it be our *fault*? I suppose we would have to say: 'Yes, it might be possible.' That said, it would be ludicrous to suggest that all human suffering, yours, mine, and that of our loved ones, must be the result of a person's specific sin—as if God punishes us all in the way he did with this man.

In fact, to our great relief, John's gospel will make that point clear when Jesus and his disciples encounter another man with a physical handicap. John writes:

As he passed by, he saw a man blind from birth. And his disciples asked him, 'Rabbi, who sinned, this man or his parents, that he was born blind?' Jesus answered, 'It was not that this man sinned, or his parents, but that the works of God might be displayed in him.'[4]

I hope this truth will be of some comfort to those of you who are suffering, even now. For while there may be occasions when we are suffering as a direct consequence of our sin, and perhaps that was even the case for the man at the pool, more often it is simply the result of living in a fallen world, a place where disease and death run rampant through the streets. Natural disasters just happen. And those who suffer as a result of them do not do so because of their sin.

SUFFERING AND THE QUESTION OF FEAR

Other implications stem from these final words to the man that are also worthy of our consideration. His last line to the man at the pool was this: 'Sin no more, that nothing worse may happen to you.' We are right to ask, 'Really? Is there anything worse than a life of suffering? Worse than spending thirty-eight years as an invalid? Isn't our health life's supreme good?' Put on edge: 'Jesus, can you give me one good reason for following you if you won't heal me?' The above questions are as profound as any we might ask.

According to what Jesus told the man at the pool, there is something worse that can befall us. Something more dreadful than a lifetime of pain. There is something even greater to *fear*. 'And what might that be?' We only need to glance down the page of John's gospel a few verses to find out. There, John records Jesus as saying:

'Truly, truly, I say to you, an hour is coming, and is now here, when the dead will hear the voice of the Son of God, and those who hear will live. For as the Father has life in himself, so he has granted the Son also to have life in himself. And he has given him authority to execute judgment, because he is the Son of Man. Do not marvel at this, for an hour is coming when all who are in the tombs will hear his voice and come out, those who have done good to the resurrection of life, and those who have done evil to the resurrection of judgment.'

Wow. If we ever wanted to consider what can be worse than suffering thirty-eight years as an invalid, this is it. Here Jesus reminds us of a final judgment, of a day when *he* will execute judgment on everyone who has ever lived. Those who honor him in this life will be given eternal life. And those who don't will be raised to a resurrection of judgment. Throughout the New Testament, this fact is acknowledged and taught by Jesus—side by side with his emphasis on love. Even the Hebrew Scriptures convey this same idea.

Evidently, this idea of being *made well* is serious business. For the man at the pool, and for you and me: If we reject Jesus now, we will be rejected by him on the final day. To put it in the simplest of terms, God is gracious, but he has also given the gavel to his son. And this very Jesus has the power to dismiss us from the presence of God for evermore. Therefore, we would be foolish to consider giving our lives over to Jesus merely for what he can do for us in the present. His work on our behalf extends into eternity.

These are tough, but important, truths for anyone who feels betrayed by God in this life. In one sense, they unmask the futility of our imagined power, the one thing we like to think our sufferings offer to us over God: leverage. We like control. The power that says God owes us something. Yet, in light of Jesus' last words with us, any leverage we think we have will prove useless in the end. We simply won't be able to hold the sufferings of this life against God. In point of fact, and here perhaps is the application for us, we must let go of the leverage we think our sufferings give us over God. Why does John ask us to believe in Jesus even though this life has been difficult? The answer, in part, is this: because Jesus came and suffered and died to put an end to the power of sin and because the next life is forever. That's why.

SUFFERING AND THE QUESTION OF FINALITY

Of course, someone may say, 'This idea in the Christian message, that Jesus will return one day in judgment—and that on that day he will put an end to suffering—is all well and good. But if God were truly good, would he not put an end to it now? Why wait? Goodness demands *finality*!'

This question is important, and although not answered directly in the conversation Jesus has with the man at the pool, it deserves some response. Helpfully, the Bible does address it elsewhere:

> *The Lord is not slow about his promise [to return] as some count slowness, but is patient toward you, not wishing that any should perish, but that all should reach repentance.*[5]

Did you catch the logic in the reason behind God's delay in bringing evil to account, to a final end? A desire that you and I should not perish. Could it be that God, in his infinite mercy, is willing to put up with evil in hope of saving you and me from his impending judgment?

Think of it. Suppose you or I were God, and we determined to rid the world of evil now. Would we not also have to rid the world of the possibility of evil? And if so, would any of us still be here? Don't each of us possess the capacity to do harm? Perhaps we ought to be grateful that evil has not come to its complete and final end just yet, so that there is still a possibility that we might be saved!

This short book has tackled a few important questions related to suffering. Whether it be on the *first* origins of evil, the issue of *fairness* or the question of who is at *fault*, we have seen that there may be something greater to *fear*, and even why evil has not yet come to a *final* end. Only one more question remains in this conversation on human suffering, and it is one for you.

SUFFERING AND A QUESTION FOR YOU

What will you do with Jesus? In light of this conversation on suffering, how will you respond to the Christian message? Perhaps the best thing I can do to help you think your way clear on this is to take you back to the beginning, to the first words of Jesus, and ask, 'Do you want to get well?' Do you really want the fullness of what Jesus has to offer you? That is, do you want to be set straight spiritually, or just physically? And if so, are you prepared to take up the moral obligations that come along with that? After all, they are more demanding than carrying the mat the man at the pool had been on for all those years. Are you ready for all that?

I sincerely hope so. I hope that you want to be free of the bitterness that comes with hopelessness brought on by unbelief. Three things:

* First, begin looking to Jesus for more than physical relief in this present age. You must want to be made spiritually fit and morally upright. And only Jesus can do that.

* Second, release the leverage you so determinedly hold over God. Although

you may want to look him in the eye and have a long talk with him about how unfairly you were treated, remember this: He will have the last word. He will want to know what you ended up doing with his Son.

 Third, start your own conversation with God by praying:

Our Heavenly Father, I confess my sin to you. For never have I given my whole self to following your ways, or to leaning on the sufferings of your Son as payment for my iniquities. Today, I want to make a fresh start. I know, deep down, that you have not betrayed me, nor forsaken me. You are good, gracious, and have always had my eternal best interest in mind, regardless of the pain you have put before me in this life. Give me your spirit that I might have your strength. Give me a willingness to take up my

cross daily and to follow you. And give me a seat at your table, on the final day when all evil, and suffering, must thankfully, and finally, be condemned by the coming of your Son. In Jesus' name I pray, Amen.

Let me encourage you, if you have prayed that prayer, to tell a Christian friend what you have done. Then, 'get on your feet,' and find a church that believes these same things. They can help you make progress in your faith.

JOHN 5:1-15

¹ After this there was a feast of the Jews, and Jesus went up to Jerusalem. ² Now there is in Jerusalem by the Sheep Gate a pool, in Aramaic called Bethesda, which has five roofed colonnades. ³ In these lay a multitude of invalids—blind, lame, and paralyzed. ⁵ One man was there who had been an invalid for thirty-eight years. ⁶ When Jesus saw him lying there and knew that he had already been there a long time, he said to him, 'Do you want to be healed?' ⁷ The sick man answered him, 'Sir, I have no one to put me into the pool when the water is stirred up, and while I am going another steps down before me.' ⁸ Jesus said to him, 'Get up, take up your bed, and walk.' ⁹ And at once the man was healed, and he took up his bed and walked. Now that day was the Sabbath. ¹⁰ So the Jews said to the man who had been healed, 'It is the Sabbath, and it is not lawful for you to take up your bed.' ¹¹ But he answered them, 'The man who healed me, that man said to me, "Take up your bed, and walk."' ¹² They asked him, 'Who is the man who said to you, "Take up your bed and walk"?' [13] Now the man who had been healed did not know who it was, for Jesus had withdrawn, as there was a crowd in the place. [14] Afterward Jesus found him in the temple and said to him, 'See, you are well! Sin no more, that nothing worse may happen to you.' [15] The man went away and told the Jews that it was Jesus who had healed him.

ENDNOTES

1. Simone Weil, *Waiting for God*, (New York: HarperCollins, 1951), 70.

2. Elie Wiesel, *Night*, (trans. M. Wiesel; New York: Hill and Wang, 1958), 65-66.

3. This man's encounter with Jesus can be found in full by reading John 5:1-15. I encourage you to read it. The text can be found on pages 55-56. Unless otherwise marked, all subsequent quotations are from this passage.

4. John 9:1-3.

5. 2 Peter 3:9.

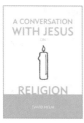

WITH **JESUS** SERIES

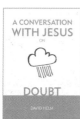

A CONVERSATION WITH JESUS ON DOUBT

9781527103283

A CONVERSATION WITH JESUS ON HOPE

9781527103290

A CONVERSATION WITH JESUS ON... BOXSET

9781527103238